Comfort My People

❧

Rowina Stanley

Comfort My People, Second Edition

Cover design by Grant Stanley (www.pixelperfekt.co.za)
Printed and bound by Shumani Mills

ISBN 978-0-620-51202-2

Yeshua Hamashiach said in **Matthew 5:17,**

"Do not think that I have come to abolish the Law
or the Prophets;
I have not come to abolish them but to fulfill them.
I tell you the truth, until heaven and earth disappear,
not the smallest letter, not the least stroke of a pen,
will by any means disappear from the Law until
everything is accomplished.
Anyone who breaks one of the least of these
commandments and teaches others to do the same
will be called least in the kingdom of heaven,
but whoever practises and teaches these commands
will be called great in the kingdom of heaven.
For I tell you that unless your righteousness surpasses
that of the Pharisees
and the teachers of the law,
you will certainly not enter the kingdom of heaven"

In Yeshua, the former things in the Old Testament are fulfilled and this includes the destiny of the nation of Israel and the Jewish people! Thus the saying that, "the New Testament is in the Old Testament concealed and the Old Testament is in the New Testament revealed", proves itself to be true as we consider the words of our Saviour in **Matthew 5:17**.

The nation of Israel is essential to the return of Jesus Christ, since it is He who sorrowfully cried out to the Jews at the time; *"I tell you, you will not see me again until you say, 'Blessed is He who comes in the name of the Lord!"* **Luke 13:35**

The restoration of Zion is seen as a prelude to the return of the Lord in glory: *"For the LORD will rebuild Zion and appear in his glory"*. **Psalm 102:16**

At a time such as this, as we witness the manifestation of many Old Testament prophecies concerning Israel and those prophecies proclaimed by our Lord concerning the last days in **Matthew 24** and **Luke 21**, come to pass, God is doing a glorious thing upon this earth, He is raising up a standard of prayer for Israel and the nations through the church! Can you see it?

God is calling upon the church to stand in the gap for Israel as never before and to carry her in prayer until the appointed time of our Lord's return! In order to pray effectively for Israel we need to pray God's Word concerning them, since His word teaches us what to pray with an amazing promise that He watches after His Word to fulfil it! **Jer.1:12**

May the Lord richly bless you as you obey God's call and stand in the gap for Israel!

"I will bless those who bless you, and whoever curses you I will curse; and all peoples on earth will be blessed through you."
Gen 12:3

CONTENTS

Prologue

I n 2007 whilst still employed in my secular job I felt a strong burden in my heart to go into fulltime counselling. I indicated my intentions to my employer during the course of the year and with his approval I was able to work up until the end of March 2008. 'My plans' were to complete a two year certificate course in Community Counselling at a local Christian Bible College.

However, during the last quarter of 2007 a desire to visit Israel so overwhelmed me that I put the other passion on hold and started entertaining this desire to visit Israel first. (I now know that my sudden change of plans was partly as a result of much intercession that took place at the Carmel Assembly on Mt Carmel Haifa for volunteers at their Beit Yedidia guest house, and that it was God who had redirected 'my plans'). Visiting Israel has always been a life long desire of mine, however I just did not know that 2008 would be the year that it would materialise.

I sought the face of the Lord in this regard since I needed to be sure whether this desire was from the Him or not. I received three very clear and precise scriptures from the Lord . On the 15th January 08' He spoke to me through **Isaiah 41v13**, *"For I am the Lord your God, who takes hold of your right hand and says to you, do not fear; I will help you"*. On the 8th February I received my second confirmation in **Exodus 23v20**, *"See, I am sending my angel before you to lead you safely to the land I have prepared for you"*. I was totally overwhelmed by the final confirmation I received on 5th March in **2 Samuel 7v3**, *"Go, do all that is in your heart, for the Lord is with you"*.

That settled it for me and I can most certainly testify that God did help me, that He did send His angels ahead of me and that I was able to do all that was in my heart to do.

I started this journey by making enquiries about possible volunteer jobs in Israel, since this option would allow me to stay for at least three months, and I was once again amazed at how God directed my footsteps. The door was opened for me through an enquiry I made in this regard to the editor of a Messianic magazine I receive on a quarterly basis. He referred me to a fellow South African, residing in Israel for some time, who in turn was the channel God used to link me to the open door at Beit Yedidia Mt.Carmel, Haifa.

My experience here was more than I could ever have hoped for and I am eternally grateful to the Lord for His faithfulness towards me during this season in my life. I was able to serve and fellowship with God's people in new and fulfilling ways. As a volunteer, resident at Beit Yedidia, I was able to serve in this vineyard with believers from different nations and fellowship with them when time allowed me to. The Messianic worship at the Kehilat Carmel Assembly on Shabbat was an amazing experience, as was all the other activities that I was able to be part of as a volunteer. I was able to meet and serve believers from different nations as they passed through the doors of Beit Yedidia, the guest house.The excellent bus service in Israel allowed me on my off days, to travel to places like Jerusalem in the south and Akko in the north with ease and the comfort of these buses made me feel like a very special tourist every time.

The relationships built in this short period of time and the few short visits to the old city of Jerusalem are at the top of my most memorable experiences and there are many. But I guess the defining moment for me was the hour or more spent in the mornings with fellow intercessors in the basement hall at Beit Yedidia, where we worshipped our Lord and sought His face!. What a privilege it was to stand in the gap for the nation of Israel and other nations with Senior Pastor David Davis, intercessors from the congregation and volunteers from other nations. It was here that the Holy Spirit birthed the following assignments upon my heart; to make Israel the first fruit of my daily intercession and to encourage as many believers back home to pray for Israel!

At the beginning of May '09 the Holy Spirit impressed the third leg of God's assignment upon my heart, namely to write a book on prayer for Israel entitled 'Comfort my people'! This was always going to be an extremely challenging assignment, since even though I enjoy writing, I had never considered writing a book before! But praise be to God that He, who knows everything about us, had equipped me in the ministry of prayer through many seasons in preparation for this assignment!

In 1995 I joined the intercessory prayer group at our local church, in operation for about a year then, from 5am to 6am Monday to Friday, to intercede for the lost, God's people and their needs, the local community with all its problems, our government and the many other areas of prayer that the Holy Spirit would burden us with! We now witness the fruit of these prayers in the community of Woodstock which is currently being transformed before our very eyes into a flourishing and now much sought after area, for various trade markets and businesses. The transformation of this once seemingly neglected community, notorious for its crime, is a testimony of what God can do as a result of unceasing and persistent intercession by faithful and committed intercessors! Numerous drug houses in the area have closed down, and former hotels and abandoned buildings illegally occupied by vagrants and those involved in drugs and prostitution, are now being revamped, providing this community with the much needed facelift and transformation that we have prayed for through the years! I praise God for the faithful and persistant prayers of the intercessors at Fountain of Joy Ministries, Woodstock with whom I was able to be a part of for many years!

How precious these times of intercession were to me especially during my own personal times of trials and testing. I lear'nt very quickly that prayer infuriates the enemy and that intercessors become his prime targets! Yes, the enemy knows that prayer moves the hand of God and one of his main objectives therefore is to keep us off our knees! In May 1995 my eleven year old daughter was diagnosed with cancer and a year later, my eldest son, at university at the time, got hooked onto drugs which lasted for about seven years. But after many months of chemo therapy treatment and a successful operation, my daughter was declared cancer free after a ten year remission period! Praise be to God who answers prayer! My son was supernaturally delivered from his addiction right in our home, all as a result of prayer! It was during this time that my relationship with my dad, which had been strained for many years was restored, and I witnessed victory after victory in many other areas of my life! **I've learnt that there is no more powerful place to be than on your knees before an Almighty God!**

A couple of years later I was asked to lead the prayer ministry of our church, which I did with God's help and with much joy and passion up until the end of 2007. I praise God that by His grace I can continue to be a watchman on the walls of Jerusalem, our nation and the nations of the World!

Acknowledgements

All glory to Abba Father God who has entrusted me with this assignment! All praise to the Holy Spirit, my counsellor and teacher who has guided me all the way. All honor to my Lord, Saviour and Redeemer Yeshua Hamashiach whose sacrifice on Calvary has opened the door for me as a child of God to be of service to Him in a manner such as this.

I praise the Lord who saw it fit to expose me to the prophetic ministry at the Carmel Assembly, which has deepened my understanding with regard to God's Word concerning Israel and also how to pray more effectively for this nation.

I thank the Lord for the opportunity allowed to me to intercede with someone like Pastor David Davis whose insight, knowledge and understanding of God's Word, past history and current affairs concerning Israel has been instrumental in deepening my understanding concerning all these areas of prayer. As he imparted these precious nuggets and insight concerning Israel in the morning prayers, unbeknown to him, I was literally absorbing them like a vacuum cleaner and storing them like precious stones within the walls of my heart.

My life has been enriched, my insight deepened, my understanding broadened and my knowledge of the Lord increased as a result of the door that He had opened for me!

To God be all the praise, honor and glory!

Dedication

I dedicate this book to the faithful
intercessors of Fountain of Joy Ministries
Woodstock, with whom I had the privilege
of seeking God's face for many years
through good times and bad, summer
and winter on the mountain tops and
in the valleys of our own personal lives,
on behalf of families, communities and
nations. What a privilege it was to co-
labour with our Lord in the ministry of
intercession in the early hours of the
morning! My prayer for you is that
"our Lord would remember all your sacrifices
and accept all your burnt offerings,
May He give you the desires of your heart
and make all your plans succeed".
(Psalm 20:3-4)

Introduction

*T*here are many books on the shelves of Christian book stores covering the subject of prayer but I have not as yet come across a book on prayer specifically for Israel in our local bookstores! So I asked the Holy Spirit for clear guidelines with regard to this prayer guide and the Holy Spirit impressed upon my heart to address the following three areas namely;

Why do we as believers have to pray for Israel,

when do we have to pray for Israel, and

what do we pray, when praying for Israel?

Well, one thing I have learnt is that not all believers have a burden of prayer for Israel and that God seems to work with remnants to achieve His purposes so that

He receives the glory in the end. I see this pattern in the battles fought by Israel in the old Testament that have been won with just a remnant and even the battle for the modern day nation of Israel prior and after independence in 1948, when all God used to accomplish His purposes and victory for Israel was a remnant!

Now, as the time of our Lord's return draws even closer, I believe God is not wanting just a remnant of believers to intercede for Israel any longer as has been the case in the past, (**Isaiah: 62v6**) but He is calling the Bride of Christ (the Church) (**Rev: 21v9)** to rise up and give ourselves no rest as we pray for the Wife of God (Israel) (**Jer: 31v32)** until Jerusalem becomes the praise of the earth!

God is calling the church, as the days of tribulation fast approaches, to raise up the arms of Israel in prayer, as the arms of Moses was raised up by Aaron and Hur when confronted by the enemy which resulted in them being victorious both in the spiritual realm and on the battle field. God is raising up a standard of prayer for the Jews across the nations as never before as a shield against the intensified attacks of the enemy.

This I believe is our assignment from Abba God's heart for Israel as the Body of Christ, to intercede for her as the Holy Spirit leads us and as God's Word teaches us and to utilize our weapons of warfare (**2Cor: 10v4-5**) on her behalf and take hold of the authority that is ours in Christ Jesus (**Matthew: 18v18**) to bind the works of the enemy and demolish every stronghold that would set itself up against the knowledge of God. Since God's Word teaches us that our battles are realy a spiritual battle and not against flesh and blood (**Eph: 6v12**), we should then understand that the battle for Jerusalem and Israel is ultimately a spiritual one. As the enemy intensifies his attacks against Israel in these last days on all fronts and through nations that seek to destroy her, (**Psalm: 83v4**) we as the church need to intensify our intercession on her behalf until God's appointed end time for the church has come and God Himself comes to her rescue in His divine and powerful way as recorded in the prophetic books of Ezekiel, Daniel, Zechariah, Revelation and others!

A wonderful illustration of a non Jew's support, love and commitment to a Jew is to be found in the well known story of Ruth and Naomi. Ruth a Moabite women committed herself fully to her assignment of caring for her mother-in-law Naomi after both daughters in law lost their spouses, which left Ruth with no obligation realy to remain committed to Naomi. Whilst the other daughter-in-law Orpah took the gap, Ruth stood firm in her comittment and assignment by assuring Naomi of her love with these wonderful words, *"Where you go I will go, and where you stay I will stay, Your people will be my people and your God my God. Where you die I will die, and there I will be buried. May the LORD deal with me, be it ever so severely, if anything but death separates you and me"*. **Ruth: 1v16-17**

Could we stand in the gap and commit ourselves to this assignment from the Lord, understanding that nothing on earth can do what prayer does, since it is prayer that moves the hand of God. This commitment will not only bless the heart of our Heavenly Father but great will be our reward since God Himself says, *"I will bless those who bless you and whoever curses you I will curse; and all peoples on the earth will be blessed through you."* **Genesis: 12v3**

Why do we as believers have to pray for Israel:

I have no doubt there are still many Christians who would ask this question. Many may still be of the opinion that the church has replaced the Jews because of their rebellion against God and rejection of Jesus Christ as the Messiah and have therefore forfeited their covenant relationship with God. But God is a covenant keeping God and declares in **Malachi: 3v6-7,** *"I the LORD do not change .... Return to me, and I will return to you",* says the LORD Almighty.

The apostle Paul in the book of **Romans II** addresses this very train of thought and leaves us in no doubt that God has not forsaken the Jews and that they are still very much part of His plan of salvation. In fact God's Word in this chapter reminds us that the Jews are the root that supports us, the wild olive shoot and that because of their transgression salvation has come to the Gentiles. Paul goes on to inform us in **verse 25-26** that *"Israel has experienced a hardening in part until the full measure of Gentiles has come in. And so all Israel will be saved ....."*

In the gospel of **John: 4v22-23,** Jesus told the Samaritan woman; *"You Samaritans worship what you do not know; we worship what we do know for salvation is from the Jews. Yet a time is coming and has now come when the true worshippers will worship the Father in spirit and truth, for they are the kind of worshippers the Father seeks. God is Spirit and His worshippers must worship in spirit and in truth."*

With regard to the above scripture, Derek Prince, the founder and director of the Derek Prince Ministry and lover of Israel who has since gone to be with the Lord, often mentions in his books and newsletters the fact that every spiritual blessing we ever received we owe to one nation, the Jewish people. He illustrates this by reminding his readers that if there had been no Jews, there would be no patriarchs, no prophets, no apostles, no Bible and no Saviour. I certainly have no argument against this!

In the book of **Ephesians** the apostle Paul clarifies the truth that in Jesus Christ the Jew and Gentile have become one new man. *"For he himself is our peace, who has made the two one and has destroyed the barrier, the dividing wall of hostility, by abolishing in his flesh the law with its commandments and regulations. His purpose was to create in himself one new man out of the two, thus making peace, and in this one body to reconcile both of them to God through the cross, by which he put to death their hostility."* (**Eph: 2v14-16**)

The above mentioned scriptures leaves me in no doubt as to our obligation to pray for Israel and Jews all over the world as we would pray for our own families and fellow believers in Christ!

Here are some of the scriptures in God's word that calls upon us very clearly to pray for Israel;

Isaiah: 40v1-5; *"Comfort, comfort my people,"* *says your God. "Speak tenderly to Jerusalem, and proclaim to her that her hard service has been completed."*

One of the most powerful ways of comforting Israel is through prayer! We may not always be able to give of our resources or serve in the nation but we can pray at all times!

Isaiah: 62v6-7; *"You who call on the LORD, give yourselves no rest, and give Him no rest till He establishes Jerusalem and makes her the praise of the earth."*

Do we as believers call on the name of the LORD? Of course we do or should be doing if we are God's children. Therefore this instruction is most definitely meant for us!

Psalm:122v6-9; *"Pray for the peace of Jerusalem:May those who love you be secure.*

May there be peace within your walls and security within your citadels."

This psalm not only instructs us to pray but what to pray and with a blessing of security as a reward!

Ezekiel:22v30; *"I looked for a man among them who would build up the wall and stand before me in the gap on behalf of the land so I would not have to destroy it, but I found none."*

God is even now seeking for intercessors whose prayers would be like a shield for Israel, prayers that will bring her to repentance, prayers that would sustain her and keep her until God's appointed time of complete restoration.

When do we have to pray for Israel?

The scriptures below make a strong appeal for our unceasing prayers for Israel.

Isaiah:62v1; *"For Zion's sake I will not keep silent, for Jerusalem's sake I will not remain quiet, till her righteousness shines out like the dawn, her salvation like a blazing torch"*

v6; *"I have posted watchmen on your walls, O Jerusalem; they will never be silent day or night".*

Psalm:137v5-6; *"If I forget you, O Jerusalem, may my right hand forget its skill. May my tongue cling to the roof of my mouth if I do not remember you, if I do not consider Jerusalem my highest joy."*

Isaiah:66v10; *"Rejoice with Jerusalem and be glad for her, all you who love her; rejoice greatly with her, all you who mourn over her."*

I once again quote Derek Prince when he encourages believers how to pray for Israel, "We are to be the Lord's secretaries, reminding Him, Lord, remember you promised to Abraham, Isaac and Israel. Remember what Jesus said about Jerusalem? Remember, remember, remember. In other words, we are holding God to His own commitment to Jerusalem. This is the most powerful form of intercession we can practise. It says, "God, You said. We hold You to Your word. We will not keep quiet. We will not stop praying until You do what You said." End of quote!

With these words in mind let me guide you through the specific way I was led by the Holy Spirit as to what to pray for Israel at a time such as this! Are these prayers for Israel very different from those that have been prayed by faithful intercessors throughout the ages? I guess not! But this much I know and that is that in the best of times and the worst of times God had always raised up a standard prayer for Israel, since it is the intercession of God's people through the ages that has preceded His divine intervention on behalf of those prayed for! I recall too well the passionate intercession of Daniel and Nehemiah that brought about victory and success in their day.

In **Matthew:5v17;** Jesus Christ says the following, *"Do not think that I have come to abolish the Law or the Prophets; I have not come to abolish them but to fulfill them".*

In **John:1v17;** the apostle shares with us this wonderful truth, *"For the law was given through Moses; grace and truth came through Jesus Christ!"*

As I sought God's guidance for the outline and content for this book, the guidance given by our Lord to the disciples in Matthew 6v9 as to how to pray, was impressed upon my heart and it is this blueprint that will be used as a guideline as we pray for Israel. For the law that was given to Moses is fulfilled through the grace provided in Jesus Christ and it is only through this grace that we are able to obey God's commandments as they apply to our own lives today. For the Jews then and now, the law, in the absence of this grace in Christ, became a yoke that they could not carry, but God in His infinite mercy and compassion makes this grace available so that we all can, both Jew and non Jew live lives of obedience to God through this grace that is ours in Yeshua Hamashiach our Lord!

As you intercede I trust you will appreciate this grace that is ours in Christ Jesus our Lord which I believe is revealed so beautifully in what we know as the Lords prayer!

As you pray I trust it will be with a heart filled with compassion for a people whose lives have constantly been threatened with annihilation from the days of the patriarchs up to now, by individuals, empires and modern day nations around her harboring terrorists and organizations who still view her as the enemy to be wiped off the map of the world . But praise God none of them have been successful in their evil schemes because of God's divine covenant with her! **Exodus 6:1-8.** All her enemies, including Pharoah, Haman, Herod and Hitler perished and with God's help she has been able to win every battle against her since being established as the nation of Israel in 1948. God's Word proves itself to be true every time that *"no weapon forged against you will prevail, and you will refute every tongue that accuses you."* **Isaiah 54:17.**

As we pray let us remember that the battle for Jerusalem and Israel is primarily a spiritual one and that this city, the center of the world is the focus of God's purpose on earth and concerns the return of Jesus Christ to set up His Kingdom on earth. All the conflict in and controversy surrounding this nation has nothing to do with politics but has everything to do with Satan's plan to destroy that which is fundamental to the return of our Lord and Saviour Jesus Christ.

Satan's battle is realy against God Himself and His creation and his aim is to destroy the plans and purposes of God and the fullness thereof which ultimately climaxes in the return of Jesus Christ to earth. The opposition to Jerusalem being the capitol of the Jewish state of Israel is realy opposition to the return of Jesus Christ! This spiritual battle which manifests itself in the physical realm in the attacks by its enemies is in reality attacks on God himself and His plans of salvation for the house of Israel!

Therefore since this battle for Jerusalem and against the nation of Israel is realy a spiritual one, we who call upon the Name of the Lord and who have the spiritual weapons of warfare at our disposal should be relentless in our prayer for the root of our faith!

The prayers and praises in this prayer guide are accompanied by but a few of the many scriptures relating to the nation of Israel and it's people in God's Word!

"You shall not have no other gods before me"
(Deut 5:7) – LAW

Jesus said, *"Worship the Lord your God , and serve Him only"*.
(Matt 4:10)

"Our Father in heaven"
(Matt 6:9) – GRACE

"Our Father in heaven" affirms personal relationship with God and recognises Him as Lord over all.
LASB (NIV)

❧⚜☙

The Israelites were never able to fully obey God as is revealed in the Bible to us. God yearned for them to love **(Deut 6:4-5)** and obey Him **(Deut 5:29)** in all of their ways.

In **Isaiah 46:9-10**, God announces that which sets Him apart from all other gods, namely, *"I am God, and there is no other; I am God, and there is none like me. I make known the end from the beginning, from ancient times, which is still to come"*.
.

Praise God for His everlasting covenant with the Jewish people and for establishing them in the land He had promised their forefathers. *"The whole land of Canaan, where you are now an alien, I will give as an everlasting possession to you and your descendants after you; and I will be their God"* **(Genesis 17:8)**

Praise God that He had revealed Himself to the Jews when they cried out to Him and remained faithful and committed to them inspite of their rebellion. *"Nevertheless my* *lovingkindness will I not utterly take from him, nor suffer my faithfulness to fail. My covenant will I not break, nor alter the thing that is gone out of my lips".* **(Psalm 89:33-34)**

Praise God that He has proved Himself to be a mighty deliverer, provider, sustainer and protector of His people through all the ages. *"Blessed be the Lord, that hath given rest unto His people Israel, according to all that he promised: there hath not failed one word of all his good promises".* **(1Kings 8:56)**

Loosen them from the spirit of rebellion and unbelief

Pray for God's mercy and compassion for His people. *"The LORD, the LORD, the compassionate and gracious God, slow to anger, abounding in love and faithfulness, maintaining love to thousands, and forgiving wickedness, rebellion and sin".*(**Exodus 34:6-7**)

Pray that the scales would fall from their eyes and veils from their hearts. *"Immediately something like scales fell from Saul's eyes and he could see again".* **(Acts 9:18)** *"'Even to this* *day when Moses is read, a veil covers their hearts. But whenever anyone turns to the Lord, the veil is taken away".* **(2Cor 3:15-16)**

Pray that they would repent from their rebellion even now and turn to God their Father! *"If my people, who are called by my name, will humble themselves and pray and seek my face and turn from their wicked ways, then will I hear from heaven and will forgive their sin and will heal their land".* **(2Chron 7:14)**

Pray that their hearts of stone would be turned to hearts of flesh and receptive to the Word of God! *"I will give you a new heart and put a new spirit in you; I will remove from you your heart of stone and give you a heart of flesh".* **(Ezekiel 36:26)**

"You shall not make for yourself an idol in the form of anything in heaven above or on the earth below. You shall not bow down to them; for I, the LORD your God, am a jealous God, punishing the children for the sin of the fathers to the third generation of those who hate me, but showing love to a thousand generations of those who love me and keep my commandments"
(Deut 5:8-10) - LAW

Jesus said, *"No servant can serve two masters"*
(Luke 16:13)

"Hallowed be your name"
(Matt 6:8) - GRACE

"Hallowed be your name", honors God as sacred, holy, majestic, splendid and powerful.
LASB (NIV)

Many Jews are still caught up in idolatry of various kinds and not worshipping the one and only true God. Many are caught up in the mysticism of the Kabala, the humanism of the Haskala, the New Age Movement, Buddahism and others.

"So therefore watch yourselves very carefully, so that you do not become corrupt and make for yourselves an idol, an image of any shape, whether formed like a man or woman, or like any animal on earth or any bird that flies in the air, or like any creature that moves along the ground or any fish in the waters below". **(Deut 4:15-18)**

Loosen them from their affiliations to false religions and all forms of idolatry!

Bind their wills to the Will of God.

Praise God that He is a holy God and that there is no other God beside Him! *"For I am the LORD your God, the Holy One of Israel, your Saviour"* **(Isaiah 43:3)**

Praise God that He had set Israel apart to be holy unto Him! *"You are to be holy to me because I, the LORD, am holy, and I have set you apart from the nations to be my own"*. **(Lev 20:26)**

Pray that the Jews would seek God with all their hearts! *"You will seek me and find me when you seek me with all your hearts"* **(Jer 29:13)**

Pray that they would walk in reverent fear of the Lord. *"Oh, that their hearts would be inclined to fear me and keep all my commands always, so that it might go well with them and their children forever"* **(Deut 5:29)** *"Fear the LORD your God, serve Him only and take your oaths in His name"*. **(Deut 6:13)**

Pray that they would love the Lord with all their hearts, soul and strength. *"Love the LORD your God with all your heart and with all your soul and with all your strength"* **(Deut 6:5)**

Pray that they would remember and acknowledge the God of Abraham, Isaac and Jacob as the One who had promised to establish them as a nation and give them life. *"When I brought them into the land flowing with milk and honey, the land I promised on oath to their forefathers, and when they eat their fill and thrive, they will turn to other gods and worship them, rejecting me and breaking my covenant"* **(Deut 31:20)**

"For the LORD is your life, and he will give you many years in the land he swore to give to your fathers, Abraham, Isaac and Jacob" **(Deut 30:20)**

"You shall not misuse the name of the LORD your God for the LORD will not hold anyone guiltless who misuses his name"
(Deut 5:11) – LAW

Jesus said, *"Do not swear at all: either by heaven, for it is God's throne...*
(Matt 5:34)

"Your Kingdom come"
(Matt 6:10) – GRACE

"Your Kingdom come", accepts God's right to rule in our lives and His kingdom principles to govern our lives!
LASB (NIV)

Through their disobedience to the LORD the Israelites had rejected God's right to rule in their lives and did not walk in the ways of the LORD nor display the kingdom culture and character that would be unique to them as God's chosen people! *"For the Kingdom of God is not a matter of eating and drinking, but of righteousness, peace and joy in the Holy Spirit"* (**Romans 14:17**)

God's Kingdom demands abandonment of all other values and ends with final separation of the unrighteous from the righteous.

Loosen them from all unrighteousness and insubmissiveness!

Praise God for the privilege of having Him rule in our lives resulting in the fulfillment of His good plans and purposes for our lives. *"For I know the plans that I have for you .."* (**Jer. 29:11**)

Praise God for the wonderful benefits of the Kingdom of God that is available to His children that love and obey Him. *"plans to* *prosper you and not to harm you, plans to give you a hope and a future."* **(Jer 29:11)**

Pray that the Jews would humble themselves and make way for God's rulership in their lives. *"In righteousness you will be established; tyranny will be far from you; you will have nothing to fear".* **(Isaiah 54:14)**

Pray that they would revere and respect God's name. *"But for you who revere my name, the sun of righteousness will rise with healing in its wings"* **(Mal 4:2)**

Pray that they would hunger and thirst after righteousness. *"Blessed are those who hunger and thirst for righteousness for they will be filled".* **(Matt 5:6)**

Pray that the Jews would first seek God's kingdom and His righteousness before anything else. *"But seek first His kingdom and his righteousness, and all these things will be given to you as well"* **(Matt 6:33)**

Pray that they would make peace with God first in their hearts and pray for the peace of

Jerusalem. *"Pray for the peace of Jerusalem; May those who love you be secure. May there be peace within your walls and security within your citadels"* **(Psalm 122:6-7)**

Pray that kingdom joy would be restored to their hearts. *"Restore to me the joy of your salvation and grant me a willing spirit to sustain me".* **(Psalm 51:12)**

"Observe the Sabbath"
(Deut 5:12) – LAW

Jesus Christ said to them, *"The Sabbath was made for man, not man for the Sabbath. So the Son of Man is Lord of the Sabbath".*
(Mark 2:27)

"Your will be done..."
(Matt 6:10) – GRACE

"Your will be done" submits completely to God's will now as guide to life on earth.
LASB (NIV)

Praise God for His will that is a blessing and for His ways that are perfect. *" For my thoughts are not your thoughts, neither are your ways my ways," declares the LORD. "As the heavens are higher than the earth, so are my ways higher than your ways and my thoughts than your thoughts"*. **(Isaiah 55:8-9)**

Praise God that doing His will leads to salvation and that He will always guide us as we submit to His will for our lives.*"Whether you turn to the right or to the left, your ears will hear a voice behind you saying, "This is the way; walk in it"*. **(Isaiah 30:21)**

Loosen them from the spirit of tradition, selfrighteousness and pride.

Bind their minds to the mind of Yeshua, their wills to the Will of God and their desires to His.

Pray that they will become sensitive and obedient to the voice of the Lord, desire to walk in His ways and turn back to Him.

"Give ear and come to me; hear me, that your soul may live. I will make an everlasting covenant with you, my faithful love promised to David". **(Isaiah 55:3)**

Pray that God would fill them with the knowledge of His will. *"For this reason, since the day we heard about you, we have not stopped praying for you and asking God to fill you with the knowledge of his will through all spiritual wisdom and understanding".* **(Col 1:9)**

Pray that God would soften their partially hardened hearts so that they would become receptive to His will for their lives! *" I will give you a new heart and a new spirit in you; I will remove from you your heart of stone and give you a heart of flesh. And I will put my Spirit in you and move you to follow my decrees and be careful to keep my laws".* **(Ezekiel 36:26-27)**

Pray they would acknowledge the LORD in all their ways. *"Trust in the LORD with all your heart and lean not on your own understanding; in all your ways acknowledge Him, and He will make your paths straight".* **(Prov 3:5-6)**

Pray that God's will be done in their relationships with each other and foreigners living in Israel. *"Do not mistreat an alien or oppress him, for you were aliens in Egypt".* **(Exodus 22:21)**

"Do not deprive the alien or the fatherless of justice, or take the cloak of the widow as a pledge. Remember that you were slaves in Egypt and the LORD your God redeemed you from there. That is why I command you to do this" **(Deut 24:17-18)**

Pray that God would open up the eyes of their understanding as they read the scriptures and that His will be done in the revelation of His Word to their hearts and minds!

Your kingdom come and Your will be done in ISRAEL!

God's Word very clearly marks the boundaries of the land that he has given to the nation of Israel. In **Genesis 15: 18-21** He says, " *To your descendants I give this land, from the river of Egypt to the river, the Euphrates.* In **Genesis 17:7-8,** God says to them, *"I will establish my covenant as an everlasting covenant between me and your descendants after you for generations to come, to be your God and the God of your descendants after you. (8) The whole land of Canaan, where you are now an alien, I will give as an everlasting possession to you and your descendants after you; I will be their God."* Then again in **Exodus 23:31,** *I will establish your borders from the Red Sea to the Sea of the Philistines, and from the desert to the River."* In Deuteronomy God's word says, *"Your territory will extend from the desert to Lebanon, and from the Euphrates River to the western sea".* **(Deut 11:24)**

Even after the Jews were scattered and banished from the land of Israel and inhabited by foreigners at various intervals in history, God promised to return them to the land He had given them as an inheritance!*"However, the days are coming,"* declares the LORD, *"when men will no longer say, 'As surely as the LORD lives, who brought the Israelites up out of Egypt,' but they will say, 'As surely as the LORD lives, who brought the Israelites up out of the land of the north and out of all the countries where he had banished them.' For I will restore them to the land I gave their forefathers."* **(Jeremiah 16:14-15)**

God will gather them back to the land of Israel! *"From that day forward the house of Israel will know that I am the LORD their God. And the nations will know that the people of Israel went into exile for their sin, because they were unfaithful to me. So I hid my face from them and handed them over to their enemies, and they fell by the sword. Therefore this is what the Sovereign LORD says: I will now bring Jacob back from captivity and will have compassion on all the people of Israel and I will be jealous for my holy name. When I have brought them back from the nations and have gathered them from the countries of their enemies, I will show myself holy through* them in the sight of many nations. Then they will know that I am the LORD their God, for though I sent them into exile among the nations, I will gather them to their own land." **(Ezekiel 39:22-28)**

Praise God for His faithfulness towards the Jews and His Word that He looks after to fulfill. *"...for I am watching to see that my word is fulfilled."* **(Jeremiah 1:12)**

"As the rain and the snow come down from the heaven, and do not return to it without watering the earth and making it flourish, so that it yields seed for the sower and bread for the eater, so is my word that goes out from my mouth; It will not return to me empty, but will accomplish what I desire and achieve the purpose for which I sent it." **(Isaiah 55:10-11)**

"God is not a man, that he should lie, nor a son of man, that he should change his mind. Does he speak and then not act? Does he promise and not fulfill? **(Numbers 23:19)**

Although Israel's original borders have been somewhat changed since Genesis 15,

God's word concerning her has not, and the birth of Israel as a nation on 14th May 1948, is a testimony to the commitment of God to His word! In fact history teaches us that this nation was born in a day, which once again confirms God's prophetic word in Isaiah to be true. *"Who has ever heard of such a thing? Who has ever seen such things? Can a country be born in a day or a nation be brought forth in a moment? Yet no sooner is Zion in labor than she gives birth to her children. Do I bring to the moment of birth and not give delivery?" says the LORD. "Do I close the womb when I bring to delivery?" says your God.* **(Isaiah 66:8-9)**

Pray that the current borders of Israel would remain in tact and that there would never again be an agreement to sell any part of this land given to them by God Himself! In fact this land belongs to God! *"The land must not be sold permanently, because the land is mine and you are but aliens and my tenants".* **(Leviticus 25:23)**

Pray the Blood of Jesus Christ daily over this nation and it's people, it's borders, every mode of transport, the Sea of Galilee (Israel's main source of water) etc, since the enemy is relentless in his pursuits to destroy this nation. **(Exodus 12:23)**

Pray that God would continue to sustain and prosper this nation according to His word and that trade relationships between Israel and her trading partners will flourish and remain secure. *"Your gates will always stand open, they will never be shut, day or night, so that men may bring you the wealth of nations."* **(Isaiah 60:11)**

Pray that God's Kingdom come in every home and community in Israel and that He will indeed pour out His Spirit on all! *"And afterward, I will pour out my spirit upon all people. Your sons and daughters will prophecy, your old men will dream dreams, your young men will see visions. Even on my servants, both men and women, I will pour out my Spirit in those days!* **(Joel 2:28-29)**

Pray that God's Kingdom come in the law of the land, that as a democratic nation they would not adopt the ungodly policies and practices of other nations and that the policies allowing abortions and same sex marriages be reversed. *"Do not turn aside from any of the commands I give you today, to the right or to the left, following other gods and serving them."* **(Deut 28:14)**

Pray that the allies of Israel like the USA, the United Kingdom, Germany, France and others would remain supportive and faithful to her inspite of increasing pressure by her enemies for these allies to reject her policy against dividing Jerusalem and her stand against a two state resolution. God's word promises Israel and warns the Gentile nations that He will bring judgement on any nation that opposes His purposes of redemption and restoration for Israel! *"For the nation or kingdom that will not serve you will perish; it will be utterly ruined."* **(Isaiah 60:12)**

Pray that the relationship between Israel and Egypt remain stable and that they would grow even stronger! *'In that day there will be a highway from Egypt to Assyria. The Assyrians will go to Egypt and the Egyptians to*

Assyria. The Egyptians and Syrians will worship together. In that day Israel will be the third, along with Egypt and Assyria, a blessing on the earth. The LORD Almighty will bless them, saying, "Blessed be Egypt my people, Assyria my handiwork and Israel my inheritance." (Isaiah 19:23-25)

Pray that God would bring about reconciliation between Israelis and Palestinians and that the Palestinian people would reject Hamas. *"For he himself is our peace, who has made the two one and has destroyed the barrier, the dividing wall of hostility, by abolishing in his flesh the law with its commandments and regulations."* (Ephesians 2:14-15)

Pray that the Lord in His mercy would pour forth the latter rains and fill up all the depleted reservoirs in Israel and restore the depth of the Sea of Galilee. *"Be glad, O people of Zion, rejoice in the LORD your God, for he has given you the autumn rains in righteousness. He sends you abundant showers, both autumn and spring rains, as before."* (Joel 2:23)

Pray for the release of all captive Israeli soldiers and that the Lord would expose where they are being held captive and secure their safe return to Israel.

Your Kingdom come, Your will be done in JERUSALEM

Jerusalem which God has set in the center of the nations **(Eze 5:5)** has been the only capitol of the Jewish people both spiritually and politically and has never been the capitol of any other nation.

More importantly, God has chosen Jerusalem as the city to put His name. *"I will give one tribe to his son so that David my servant may always have a lamp before me in Jerusalem, the city where I chose to put my Name"*. **(1Kings 11:36)**

"But now I have chosen Jerusalem for my Name to be there, and I have chosen David to rule my people Israel". **(2Chron 6:6)**

Furthermore God said to Solomon, *"My eyes and my heart will always be there."* **(1Kings 9:3)**

And *"I will return to Zion and dwell in Jerusalem."* **(Zech 8:3)**

Moreover, God's word indicates that He will return the Jews to Jerusalem Himself!

"I will save my people from the countries of the east and the west. I will bring them back to live in Jerusalem; they will be my people, and I will be faithful and righteous to them as their God." **(Zech 8:7-8)**

Praise God for the city of Jerusalem where He dwells, which He protects and where His glory resides! *"And I myself will be a wall of fire around it,' declares the LORD, 'and I will be its glory within* **(Zech 2:5)**

"As the mountains surround Jerusalem, so the LORD surrounds his people both now and forevermore." **(Psalm 125:2)**

Praise God for His divine plans and purposes for Jerusalem. *"Say to the Daughter of Zion, 'See, your Saviour comes! See, his reward is with Him, and his recompense accompanies him.'"* **(Isaiah 62:11)**

However, it is this piece of 'real estate' in Israel that is the cause of all the strife in the Middle East and across the globe for that matter! No peace in Jerusalem, very little peace elsewhere! And I guess it is because it is the most sensitive part of God that is affected, namely the 'apple of His eye'! Even though God's word makes it abundantly clear about who owns the city of Jerusalem and the nation of Israel, the surrounding nations who are hostile towards Israel firmly believe that the Jews are occupying land that does not belong to them!

God Himself says, *"I am going to make Jerusalem a cup that sends all the surrounding peoples reeling. Judah will be besieged as well as Jerusalem. On that day when all nations of the earth are gathered against her, I will make Jerusalem an immovable rock for all the nations."* **(Zech 12:2-3)**

Pray for the peace of Jerusalem: *"May those who love you be secure. May there be peace within your walls and security within your citadels."* **(Psalm 122:6-7)**

Pray that righteousness and justice be established in Jerusalem. *"Righteousness and justice are the foundation of your throne; love and faithfulness go before you."* **(Psalm 89:14)**

Pray for the appointed time of God's favor upon Jerusalem. *"You will arise and have compassion on Zion, for it is time to show favor to her; the appointed time has come."* **(Psalm 102:13)**

Your Kingdom come,
Your will be done in the GOVERNMENT

God sets governments in place and He removes them! *"Praise be to the name of God for ever and ever; wisdom and power are his. He changes times and seasons; he sets up kings and deposes them."* **(Daniel 2:20-21)**

Inspite of the fact that many countries are governed by leaders that are ungodly and corrupt, God's word reveals to us that it is He who puts them in place at set times and for set seasons in order that His plans and purposes be accomplished!

The current government in Israel has been set in place by God for a time such as this! God calls us to pray for them since they are first and foremost accountable to Him!

Bind the spirit of strife, arrogance and disunity within the Israeli govenment!

Pray that the Israeli government would accept God's right to rule in their lives as leaders and His kingdom principles to govern their lives resulting in these same kingdom principles to be the foundation of all legislation in Israel.

Pray for a spirit of peace and unity to abound within the Knesset and that all members will be in one accord! *"How good and pleasant it is when brothers live together in unity! .... For there the LORD bestows his blessings, even life forevermore."* **(Psalm 133)**

Pray that God would raise up men of integrity and humility to govern in Israel. *"As for you if you walk before me in integrity of heart and uprightness, as David your father did ...."* **(1Kings 9:4)**

Pray that they would govern with pure hearts, motives and soundness of mind and not be tempted into any form of corruption. *"I will set before my eyes no vile thing. The deeds of faithless men I hate; they will not cling to me."* **(Psalm 101:3)**

Pray that the Holy Spirit would influence every decision, plan and strategy made by the government! *"Not by might nor by power, but by my Spirit," says the LORD Almighty.* (**Zech 4:6**)

Pray for the Prime Minister, that he would serve in his office with a blameless heart and that God would bless him with godly wisdom, divine insight and skillful knowledge! *"I will be careful to lead a blameless life – when will you come near to me?"* (**Psalm 101:2**)

Pray that he like David would seek the face of the Lord at all times before making any decisions concerning Israel. *"and David inquired of the LORD, "Shall I pursue this raiding party? Will I overtake them?"* (**1Samuel 30:8**)

Pray that as Prime Minister he, like Nehemiah, would not compromise with the allies or enemies concerning Jerusalem or any other land in Israel given by God to the decendants of Jacob. *"The God of heaven will give us success. We his servants will start rebuilding, but as for you, you have no share in Jerusalem or any claim or historic right to it."* (**Nehemiah 2:20**)

Pray that inspite of all the pressures he has to confront as Prime Minister in the 'hottest seat' and most volitile of places on the earth, he would remain faithful and focused and govern his people with mercy and compassion. *"For I have kept the ways of the LORD; I have not done evil by turning from my God."* **(2Samuel 22:22)**

Your kingdom come and
Your will be done in the IDF

It is God who has granted Abraham and his descendants success on the battle field time and time again as they walked in obedience to Him! Every battle plan and strategy used by the Israelites so effectively and successfully through the ages has been given to them by God Himself! From Abram's defeat of Kedorlaomer, to the collapse of Jerico's walls, from David's defeat of Goliath to Jehoshaphat's defeat of Moab and Ammon and in all the many other battle's, God has been their source of victory! *"O LORD, God of our fathers, are you not the God who is in heaven? You rule over all the kingdoms of the nations. Power and might are in your hand, and no one can withstand you. O our God, did you not drive out the inhabitants of this land before your people Israel and give it forever to the descendants of Abraham your friend?* **(2Chron 20:6-7)**

King David testifies to this fact that it is God who had provided him with the necessary skills, strength and strategies for battle. *"He trains my hands for battle; my arms can bend a bow of bronze. You armed me with strength for battle; you made my adversaries bow at my feet."* **(Psalm 18:34 & 39)**

The Israeli Defense Force has an extremely formiddable task in protecting the nation of Israel but God is still their commander in chief and their battles still belong to Him! *"This is what the LORD says to you: 'Do not be afraid or discouraged because of this vast army. For the battle is not yours, but God's.'* **(2Chron 20:15)**

Praise God that He is the protector of Israel and that His love endures forever! *"Give thanks to the LORD, for his love endures forever."* **(2Chron 20:21)**

Pray for the various divisions of the IDF, that are Israel's sword of protection against her enemies. Pray for their protection on the border posts and wherever they serve the nation of Israel. *"You are my war club, my weapon for battle – with you I shatter nations, with you I destroy kingdoms, with you I shatter* *horse and rider, with you I shatter chariot and driver, with you I shatter man and woman, with you I shatter old man and youth, with you I shatter young man and maiden, with you I shatter shepherd and flock, with you I shatter farmer and oxen, with you I shatter governments and officials."* **(Jeremiah 51:20-23)**

Pray that they would remain vigilant in the face of their enemies that are relentless in their quest to destroy them as a nation. *"Neither I nor my brothers nor my men nor the guards with me took off our clothes; each had his weapon, even when he went for water."* **(Nehemiah 4:23)**

Pray that they would not become discouraged or weary as they constantly stand in harms way against the enemies of their people! *"Don't be afraid of them. Remember the Lord, who is great and awesome, and fight for your brothers, your sons and your daughters, your wives and your homes."* **(Nehemiah 4:14)**

Pray that their methods of warfare would be above reproach and that they would not be tempted to apply unethical standards but the standards of the LORD. *'so David inquired of the LORD, and he answered, "Do not go straight up, but circle around behind them and attack them in front of the balsam trees."* **(2 Samuel 5:23)**

Pray that the young men and women serving in the IDF would fear God and honor Him and the people of Israel in their conduct and in their service! *"Thou shalt rise up before the hoary head, and honour the face of the old man, and fear thy God; I am the LORD."* **(Leviticus 19:32)**

Your will be done in returning the Exiles (ALIYAH)

The return of the Jewish people (Aliyah) to the land of Israel is an ongoing miracle! This return of the Jewish people from all four corners of the earth to Israel is another amazing testimony to the truth of God's word which He looks after to perform! *'I will say to the north, "Give them up!" and to the south, "Do not keep them back!" Bring My sons and daughters from the ends of the earth – everyone who is called by my name, whom I created for my glory, whom I formed and made.'* **(Isaiah 43:6)**

In fact God says that He will signal them! *"I will signal them and gather them in. Surely I will redeem them; they will be as numerous as before. Though I scatter them among the peoples, yet in distant lands they will remember me. They and their children will survive and they will return."* **(Zech 10:8-9)**

In line with God's Word, the Jews have indeed, through the years, been returning to Israel and more recently in greater numbers! According to resources from

Israel the Jews have returned in numbers from the former Soviet Union, North and South America, France, the United Kingdom, South Africa and Ethiopia. *"I will bring back my exiled people Israel; they will rebuild the ruined cities and live in them. They will plant vineyards and drink their wine; they will make gardens and eat their fruit. I will plant Israel in their own land, never again to be uprooted from the land I have given them." says the LORD your God.* **(Amos 9:14-15)**

According to one Israeli News Magazine the worldwide economic shaking has helped to increase aliyah in 2009 and through it the hand of the Lord God of Israel can clearly be seen.

Praise God for His faithfulness to His Word and the ongoing return of Jewish people to Israel in fulfilment of God's prophetic word

Pray that Jews still living in other nations will respond to God's signal and return to Israel!

Pray that God will make a way for them to return if they are not by the means to do so.

Pray that the settlement projects to accommodate the new immigrants (olim) will continue inspite of much opposition from inside and outside of Israel against these developments, which are considered to be illegal homes on so called 'occupied' land.

Praise God for the 'Gentiles' that have been such a blessing through the years in the area of aliyah in accordance to God's word. *"See, I will beckon to the Gentiles, I will lift up my banner to the peoples; they will bring your sons in their arms and carry your daughters on their shoulders. Kings will be your foster fathers, and their queens your nursing mothers."* **(Isaiah 49:22-23)**

Pray for organizations like Friends of Israel, ICEJ, Operation Exodus and the many other churches and organizations across the world who not only assist with Aliyah but are supporting Israel in many other ways, that the Lord would bless and sustain them and enlarge their capacity to give, support the

Jews and the nation of Israel in accordance to God's word. *"Foreigners will rebuild your walls, and their kings will serve you."* **(Isaiah 60:10)** *"Alliens will shepherd your flocks; and foreigners will work your field and vineyards."* **(Isaiah 61:5)**

Pray that God would burden many more churches across the nations with this assignment to assist the Jews with aliyah. *"Nations will take them and bring them to their own place"* **(Isaiah 14:2)**

Your will be done regarding the enemies of Israel

The enemy of Israel has manisfested itself through individuals, nations and ideologies during various periods of time in history in various ways, the most recent being that of fundamentalist Islam exposing itself in the form of terrorism across the globe. But praise God, He is never taken by surprize and this enemy too will have to bend the knee and experience the wrath of the God of Israel! In fact God's word indicates that He has created the destroyer for His purposes! *"And it is I who have created the destroyer to work havoc; No weapon forged against you will prevail and you will refute every tongue that accuses you."* (Isaiah 54:16-17)

The horrors of suicide bombings and intifadas in Israel resulting in the loss of many innocent lives, has ceased, and the nation has been enjoying some respite in this area at least in recent years. The successful containment of these onslaughts by the enemy within Israel is mainly due to the excellent strategies put in place by the Israeli government to address this problem and the tireless and outstanding work of the IDF. God's word also prophecies that their enemies would go into exile and that appears to be the case at this stage. *"But all who devour you will be devoured; all your enemies will go into exile."* **(Jeremiah 30:16)**

Bind the spirit of terrorism at work in the world today! *"Whatever you bind on earth will be bound in heaven, and whatever you loose on earth will be loosed in heaven."* **(Matthew 16:19)**

Loosen the fear of the Living God upon every terrorist!

Praise God that his word promises that, *"The scepter of the wicked will not remain over the land alloted to the righteous, for then the righteous might use their hands to do evil."* **(Psalm 125:3)**

Praise God that He promises, *"I will contend with those who contend with you, and your children I will save."* **(Isaiah 49:25)**

Pray that God would expose and paralize the works of the enemy inside and outside of Israel! *"Come", they say, "let us destroy them as a nation, that the name of Israel be remembered no more."***(Psalm 83:4)**

Pray that God would send confusion into the camps of the enemy so that they will not be able to carry out their evil plans! *"Confuse the wicked, O Lord, confound their speech, for I see violence and strife in the city."* **(Psalm 55:9)**

Pray that God would expose the lies of the enemy and nullify the false accusations contantly directed at the nation of Israel. *"This is what the Sovereign LORD says; Because people say to you, you devour men and deprive your nation of its children, therefore you will no longer devour men or make your nation childless, declares the Sovereign LORD. No longer will I make you hear the taunts of the nations, and no longer will you suffer the scorn of the peoples or cause your nation to fall, declares the Sovereign LORD."***(Ezekiel 36:13-15)**

Pray that God would totally disintegrate the structures of Hamas, Hizbollah and every other terrorist organization working towards the destruction of Israel! Pray that God would look after His word as He declares; *"Tyranny will be far from you; you will have nothing to fear. Terror will be far removed; it will not come near you. If anyone does attck you, it will not be my doing; whoever attacks you will surrender to you."* **(Isaiah 54:14-15)**

Your Kingdom come Your Will be done in the lives of the descendants of Ismael

I clearly remember being led by the Holy Spirit some years ago, whilst praying for the salvation of Muslims, to pray for the true nature of Islam be exposed. I realised some time later that this was indeed being done through the rise of terrorism.

Through the emergence of terrorism, Islam can no longer proclaim to be a religion of peace, since it is predominantly the followers of this faith who are the perpetrators of most of the acts of terrorism across the world today! However, not all followers of Islam share the fundamentalist views of the minority of those, whose choice of violence as a means to an end, has shaken the world and I have no doubt the faith of those Muslims who do not agree with the ideology of terrorism.

The spirit of rejection that has flowed through the line of Ismael since the day that he and his mother Hagar were requested to leave the tents of Abraham, his father, **(Gen 21:8-15)** remains within the hearts of his descendants today, and it is this spirit that is the root cause of all the animosity and hatred between the house of Isaac and the house of Ismael. It is this rejection that Satan is using to manipulate individuals to carry out his evil schemes to destroy the Jewish people, divide Jerusalem and ultimately God's plan of redemption which cannot exclude the Jews and the nation of Israel!

But God heard the cries of the boy, Ismael, in the desert **(Gen 21:17-20)** and came to his rescue and promised to make him into a great nation. Likewise God is hearing the cries of his descendants today, as they seek the truth and cry out to the one and only true God!

What the enemy has meant for harm, God is turning around for good! These very acts of terrorism, I believe, has removed the scales from the eyes and veils from the hearts of many of the descendants of Ismael as they become disillusioned with a faith that condones hatred, violence and terrorism!

Praise God that his desire is that all men be saved and this includes the descendants of Ismael! *"I now realise how true it is that God does not show favoritism but accepts men from every nation who fear Him and do what is right."* **(Acts 10:34-35)**

Praise God for his mercies and compassion that are new every morning towards all mankind! *"The LORD is gracious and compassionate, slow to anger and abounding in love. The LORD is good to all; he has compassion on all he has made."* **(Psalm 145:8-9)**

Loosen the descendants of Ismael from the spirit of rejection and pray that they be healed!

Bind their minds to the mind of Yeshua, their wills to the Will of God and their hearts to His!

Pray that as they seek for the truth they will find it in the one and only true God and be saved! *"You will seek me and find me when you seek me with all your heart.* **(Jeremiah 29:13)**

Ask the Lord to speak to them in dreams and visions. *"One day at about three in the afternoon he had a vision. He distinctly saw an angel of God, who came to him and said, "Cornelius."* **(Acts 10:3)**

Pray that the Lord would restore their love for their brothers. *"But Esau ran to meet Jacob and embraced him; he threw his arms around his neck and kissed him. And they wept.* **(Genesis 33:4)**

"Honor your father and your mother"
(Deut 5:16) – LAW

Jesus said, *"Anyone who loves his father and mother more than me is not worthy of me".*
(Matt 10:37)

"On earth as it is in heaven"
(Matt 6:10) - GRACE

On earth as it is in heaven means that as God and His will is honoured in heaven, so He desires it to be done on earth.
LASB (NIV)

Praise God and **honor** Him for who He is;
Elohim (God), **Yahweh** (The LORD), **El Elyon**
(God Most High), **El Shaddai** (God Almighty),
Adonai (LORD), **Yahweh Elohe Yisrael** (LORD
God of Israel), **Qedosh Yisrael** (Holy One of
Israel), **El Roi** (God Who Sees), **Yahweh Yireh**
(The LORD will Provide), **Yahweh Nissi** (The
LORD is my Banner), **Yahweh Shalom** (The
LORD is Peace), **El Olam** (The Everlasting
God), **Yahweh Tsidkenu** (The LORD our
righteousness), **Yahweh Sabaoth** (LORD
of Hosts), **Yahweh Shammah** (The LORD is
There), **Attiq Yomin** (Ancient of Days).

Praise God that He honors those who honor
Him! *"Therefore the LORD, the God of Israel,
declares: 'I promised that your house and
your father's house would minister before me
forever.' But now the LORD declares; 'Far be
it from me! Those who honor me I will honor,
but those who despise me will be disdained".*
(1Samuel 2:30)

Loosen them from the spirit of irreverance
and confusion."*The LORD will send on you*

curses, confusion and rebuke in everything you put your hand to, until you are destroyed and come to sudden ruin because of the evil you have done in forsaking him". **(Deut 28:20)**

Pray for God's mercy and compassion towards His children. *"Because of the LORD'S great love we are not consumed, for his compassions never fail. They are new every morning, great is your faithfulness."* **(Lam 3:22-23)**

Pray that they would honor God by honoring His word and obeying it. *"If you fully obey the LORD your God and carefully follow all his commands I give you today, the LORD your God will set you high above all the nations on earth."* **(Deut 28:1)**

Pray that they would submit to the LORD and give Him the honor He deserves in every area of their lives! *"The LORD your God will circumcise your hearts and the hearts of your descendants, so that you may love him with all your heart and with all your soul, and live".* **(Deut 30:6)**

Pray that those in government, the IDF (Israeli Defense Force), and in the judicial system would honor God in their service towards the nation of Israel and it's people! *"I will make known my holy name among my people Israel. I will no longer let my holy name be profaned, and the nations will know that I the Lord am the Holy One in Israel. It is coming! It will surely take place, declares the Sovereign LORD. This is the day I have spoken of."* **(Ezekiel 39:7-8)**

Pray that God would circumcise their hearts and turn their hearts fully to the Heavenly Father! *"See I will send you the prophet Elijah before that great and dreadful day of the LORD comes. He will turn the hearts of the fathers to their children, and the hearts of the children to their fathers; or else I will come and strike the land with a curse"* **(Mal 4:5-6)**

"You shall not murder"
                                    (Deut 5:17) – LAW

Jesus said, *"Anyone who is angry with his brother will be subject to judgment"*.
                                    (Matt 5:22)

"Give us today our daily bread"
                                    (Matt 6:11) – GRACE

Give us today our daily bread recognizes God's involvement in our daily lives and supplier of our daily needs.
                                    LASB (NIV)

We need God to supply us with His "daily bread" to meet our spiritual, emotional, mental and physical needs. Jesus answered the tempter by saying, *"It is written: 'Man does not live by bread alone, but on every word that comes from the mouth of God'"* **(Matt 4:4)**

We dare not lean on our own understanding and strength to obey God, since our flesh is weak and easily leads us into sin. Referring to the command *"do not murder"*, Jesus compares it to anger in **(Matt 5:22).**

Loosen them from the spirit of anger and distrust!

PRAISE God that we can trust in Him to supply us with what we need on a daily basis to live holy and victorious lives. *"So Abraham called that place The LORD Will Provide. And to this day it is said, "on the mountain of the LORD it will be provided."* **(Gen 22:14)**

Praise God that He has committed Himself to healing them from their wounds that

He had inflicted upon them and provide them the 'daily bread' they need to walk in obedience to Him. *"The moon will shine like the sun, and the sunlight will be seven times brighter, like the light of seven full days, when the LORD binds up the bruises of His people and heals the wounds he inflicted"*. **(Isaiah 30:26)**

Praise God that He restores the whole man, spiritually, physically, mentally and emotionally! *"Your wound is incurable, your injury beyond healing...... But I will restore you to health and heal your wounds"*, declares the LORD. **(Jer 30:12-17)**

Pray that the Holy Spirit would pour upon them a spirit of repentance and supplication and that they would indeed seek the LORD and cry out, *"Come, let us return to the LORD, He has torn us to pieces but He will heal us; he has injured us but he will bind up our wounds"*. **(Hosea 6:1)**

Pray that they would recognize the LORD as their healer. Ask the Lord to deliver them from all anger, which the Lord compares to murder! *"he restores my soul"* **(Psalm 23:3)**.

Ask the Lord to heal them from all brokeness! *"He heals the brokenhearted and binds up their wounds"*. **(Psalm 147:3)**

Pray that they would recognize God's hand upon them and acknowledge that He alone is their provider and that they shall not be in want when they place their trust in Him. *"The LORD is my shepherd, I shall not be in want"* **(Psalm 23:1).**

"Praise be to the Lord, to God our Saviour, who daily bears our burdens. **(Psalm 68v19)**

"You shall not commit adultery"
                    (Deut 5:18) – LAW

Jesus said, *"Anyone who looks at a woman lustfully has already committed adultery with her in his heart".*
                    (Matt 5:28)

"Forgive us our debts"
                    (Matt 6:12) – GRACE

Forgive us our debts expressess an attitude of submission and humility!
                    LASB (NIV)

God's anguish concerning the adultery of Israel is vividly described in the book of Hosea, whose own beloved wife deserts him and causes him to cry out to an unfaithful people, urging them to return to a God who loves them. History teaches us that many of the beliefs and practices of the Cannaanite religions were adopted and intergrated with worship of the Lord by the Israelites!

"Go, take for yourself an adulterous wife, because the land is guilty of the vilest adultery in departing from the LORD". **(Hosea 1:2)**

"They consult a wooden idol; and are answered by a stick of wood. A spirit of prostitution leads them astray; they are unfaithful to their God". **(Hosea 4:12)**

"She has not acknowledged that I was the one who gave her the grain, the new wine and oil, who lavished on her the silver and gold – which they used for Baal". **(Hosea 2:8)**

Loosen them from the spirit of prostitution and adultery.

Praise God that He is a God who forgives all of our sins. *"Praise the LORD, O my soul, and forget not all his benefits, who forgives all your sins and heals all your diseases, who redeems your life from the pit and crowns you with love and compassion, who satisfies your desires with good things so that your youth is renewed like the eagle's".* **(Psalm 103:2-5)**

Praise God that He has promised to heal them from their waywardness! *"I will heal their waywardness and love them freely, for my anger has turned away from them"* **(Hosea 14:4)**

Pray that they would humble themselves and submit themselves to one husband, the LORD their God! *"I will betroth you to me forever; I will betroth you in righteousness and justice, in love and compassion. I will betroth you in faithfulness, and you will acknowledge the LORD.* **(Hosea 2:19-20)**

Pray that the Holy Spirit would cleanse their hearts from all adulterous thoughts and actions and that they would desire to serve God with a pure heart! *"He who has clean hands and a pure heart, who does not lift up his soul to an idol or swear by what is false. He will receive blessing from the LORD and vindication from God his Saviour".* **(Psalm 24:4-5)**

Pray that they would be steadfast and faithful in serving God and Him alone! *"Create in me a pure heart, O God, and renew a steadfast spirit in me."* **(Psalm 51:10)**

Pray that all other relationships with family, friends and business associates etc, would be carried out with pure and upright hearts! *"The integrity of the upright guides them, but the unfaithful are destroyed by their duplicity"* **(Prov 11:3)**

"you shall not steal"
(Deut 5:19) – LAW

Jesus said, *"If someone wants to sue you and take your tunic, let him have your cloak as well"*
(Matt 5:40)

"as we also have forgiven our debtors"
(Matt 6:12) – GRACE

As we have also forgiven our debtors, expresses readiness to live as a forgiving and forgiven people.
LASB (NIV)

It is only by God's grace that we are able to resist the temptation of taking that which does not belong to us and giving to someone else that which he or she does not deserve. It is only when we fully understand God's mercy toward us and the depth thereof, that we are able to forgive others no matter the offense, no matter the cost. It is only when we completely yield ourselves to the rulership of the Holy Spirit in our lives that we are able to live lives that does not 'steal' from others anything that will cause them to be less of themselves, spiritually, emotionally, mentally and materialy. It is only as we die to self and walk in the love of Christ, that we are able to esteem others higher than ourselves, give them our 'cloaks' even whilst in the process of being sued by them!

The Israelites are a people who have been on the receiving end of much hatred, anti-semitism and plans of extermination for many centuaries. History reminds us that before and after the establishment of the state of Israel, they had endured much hardship to say the least, as individuals and as a nation, resulting in them being weary to forgive, weary to trust and weary to compromise with anything and anyone that would threaten their existence as a people again! And who can blame them!

But God's Word teaches us to do the very thing that runs contrary to our human nature and that is to forgive, even when we are the injured party, for therein lies the healing! What's more, He provides the grace for us to do so! We need only to submit and trust Him completely!

Praise God that He gives us the grace to forgive and forget and enables us to love our enemies and pray for those who persecute us! *"You have heard it said, 'Love your neighbor* **(Lev 19:18)** *and hate your enemy'. But I tell you: Love your enemies and pray for those who persecute you, that you may be sons of your Father in heaven. He causes his sun to rise on the evil and the good, and sends rain on the righteous and the unrighteous".* **(Matt 5:43-45)**

Loosen them from the spirit of bitterness and unforgiveness!

Bind their hearts to the heart of Abba Father!

Pray that the Lord would deliver them of all unforgiveness and bitterness.*"Help us, O God our Saviour, for the glory of your name; deliver us and forgive our sins for your name's sake".***(Psalm 79:9)**

Pray that the Lord would not only deliver them but heal their hearts! *"But for you who revere my name, the sun of righteousness will rise with healing in his wings. And you will go out and leap like calves released from the stall"* **(Mal 4:2)**

Pray that they would, as a nation, respond to all challenges and confrontations with hearts of righteousness and justice. *"For I, the LORD, love justice; I hate robbery and iniquity"* **(Isaiah 61:8)**

"You shall not give false testimony against your neighbor"
(Deut 5:20) – LAW

Jesus said, *"Men will have to give an account on the day of judgment for every careless word they have spoken".*
(Matt 12:36)

"And lead us not into tempatation"
(Matt 6:13) – GRACE

And lead us not into tempatation, asks for God's help in keeping us focused on Him and His purposes for our lives and not be tempted by the enemy to go astray in any area of our lives.
LASB (NIV)

౦ఞ

Nehemiah is a wonderful example of a man who remained focused upon his assignment, inspite of the opposition that came his way in the form of Sanballat and Tobiah when he pursued his passion to rebuild the walls of Jerusalem. He did not allow himself to be tempted by his enemies to forsake this project, nor did he allow himself to stoop to the level of those who falsely accused him. *"It is reported among the nations – and Geshem says it is true – that you and the Jews are plotting to revolt and therefore you are building the wall. Moreover, according to these reports you are about to become their king and have even appointed prophets to make this proclamation about you in Jerusalem: "There is a king in Judah!"* **(Neh 6:6-7)**

Nothing much has changed since the time of Nehemiah! The nation of Israel is constantly falsely accused by her enemies of being occupiers of land that was given to them by God Himself! Their efforts to protect themselves as a nation against the continual attacks of the enemy is often distorted by the anti-Israel propaganda media as being acts of violence, especially when innocent children and civilians across their borders are hurt or killed as a result of their efforts to defend themselves!

Bind that spirit of mockery and redicule against them! *"But when Sanballat the Horonite, Tobiah the Ammonite off icial and Geshem the Arab heard about it, they mocked and ridiculed us."* **(Neh 2:19)**

Praise God that He is able and willing to keep them from falling into temptation and from giving false testimony! *"For I am the LORD, your God, who takes hold of your right hand and says to you, Do not fear; I will help you".* **(Isaiah 41:13)**

Pray for strength and perseverance for the Israeli people in the face of constant physical and spiritual opposition that wears them down and tempts them to despair. *"Then Judah said, "The strength of the labourers is giving out, and there is so much rubble that we cannot build the wall".* **(Neh 4:10)**

Pray that Israel would not be tempted in any way to entertain the deceptive plans and strategies of the enemy for the sake of keeping the peace, but trust God for their victory! *"I answered them by saying, "The God of heaven will give us success. We his servants will start rebuilding, but as for you, you have no share in Jerusalem or any claim or historic right to it"* **(Neh 2:20)**

Pray that the Holy Spirit would expose the false testimonies and false accusations that are constantly being raised against Israel as being just that, false and deceptive! *"Hear us, O our God, for we are despised. Turn their insults back on their own heads. Give them over as plunder in a land of captivity. Do not cover up their own guilt or blot out their sins from your sight, for they have thrown insults in the face of the builders".* **(Neh 4:4-5)**

"You shall not covet your neighbor's wife. You shall not set your desire on your neighbor's house or land, his manservant or maidservant, his ox or donkey, or anything that belongs to your neighbor ".

(Deut 5:21) – LAW

Jesus said, *"Be on your guard against all kinds of greed".*

(Luke 12:15)

"but deliver us from the evil one"

(Matt 6:13) – GRACE

But deliver us from evil, asks for God's protection from the trials always associated with establishing God's kingdom on earth.

LASB (NIV)

King David is an example of one who succumbed to the temptation of covetousness inspite of the fact that he was an annointed king who loved the Lord and who had experienced tremendous victories over the enemies of Israel time and time again! Yet in spite of all his victories and wonderful qualities, the one whom God referred to as *'a man after my own heart'* (**1 Samuel 13:14**) & (**Acts 13:22**), fell into moral sin, reminding us that no one is exempt from succumbing to temptation and that the only protection against the schemes of the enemy is to fear God and obey Him! *"The angel of the LORD encamps around those who fear Him, and he delivers them"*. (**Psalm 34:7**)

The spirit of discontentment is one that will easily cause us to fall into moral sin and even committ murder if we do not guard our hearts against it! The consequences of greed, covetousness and discontentment is almost always devastating as was the case in King David's life. **Psalm 51** gives us an idea of the spiritual, mental and emotional pain King David endured as a result of his sin. *"Wash away all my iniquity and cleanse me from my sin. For I know my transgressions, and my sin is always before me. Against you, and you only, have I sinned and done what is evil in your sight, so that you are proved right when you speak and justified when you judge"* (**Psalm 51:2-4**)

Praise God that He is a merciful and forgiving God and that no sin is too big for Him to forgive! *"Blessed is he whose transgressions are forgiven, whose sins are covered. Blessed is the man whose sin the LORD does not count against him and in whose spirit is no deceit".* (**Psalm 32:1-2**)

Pray that the Lord would deliver them from hearts contaminated with greed, covetousness and discontentment. *"I will give them singleness of heart and action, so that they will always fear me for their own good and the good of their children after them".* (**Jer.32:39**)

Pray that the Lord would indeed deliver them from the evil one and protect them from his schemes and snares! *" Surely he will save you from the fowler's snare and from the deadly pestilence. He will cover you with his feathers, and under his wings you will find refuge; and his faithfulness will be your shield and rampart".* **(Psalm 91:3-4)**

Pray that a spirit of contentment would be their portion in all areas of their lives knowing that there is much to be gained as it is combined with a spirit of godliness. *"And godliness with contentment is great gain".* **(1Tim 6:6)**

Pray that they would not miss the blessings of the Lord in their lives and be grateful in all things!

Pray that they would rejoice in the prosperity of their neighbor and not be envious! *"Rejoice with those who rejoice"* **(Romans 12:15)**

Epilogue

*T*his book serves mainly as a prayer guide for Israel and is by no means an exposition on prayer! This assignment given by God is meant to inspire, motivate and encourage especially those believers who have not before found it necessary to pray for Israel! But I trust that it will also excite those faithful watchmen on the walls of Jerusalem, that God is now raising up an amazing standard of prayer for this nation! As a prayer guide, every need and area of prayer could not be covered, but I have no doubt that the Holy Spirit who is omnicient and faithful, will burden the intercessor with additional areas of prayer!

I have often been intriguered by the strange shape of this land and have recently received some sort of a revelation, if one can call it that, whilst reading an Israeli magazine wherein an Arab cartoonist portrayed Israel's shape as being that of a fountain pen in the hand of a writer. The message he was trying to convey was that inspite of ongoing negotiations between Israel and the Arabs regarding the land disputes, Israel writes the script and therefore no agreement will be reached! How amazing! He just did not know how close to the truth he was, since we know that it is not Israel that wrote the script but God Himself and they are within His hand!*"So do not fear, for I am with you; do not be dismayed, for I am your God. I will strengthen you and help you; I will uphold you with my righteous right hand."* **(Isaiah 41:10)**

The journey of the Jews have been a long one and their wounds been very deep! **(Jer 30:12-16)** Even their joy gone from their hearts! **(Lamentations 5:15)** But God has progressively been healing their wounds and promises to restore them completely, *"But I will restore you to health and heal your wounds"*, declares the LORD. **(Jer. 30:17).** *"I will heal their waywardness and love them freely, for my anger has turned away from them."* **(Hosea 14:4)**

As the day of our Lord's return draws ever so nearer, His word promises the following; *"And I will pour out on the house of David and the inhabitants of Jerusalem a spirit of grace and supplication. They will look at me, the one they have pierced, and they will mourn for him as one mourns for an only child, and grieve bitterly for him as one grieves for a firstborn son. On that day, the weeping in Jerusalem will be great, like the weeping of Hadad Rimmon in the plain of Megiddo."* **(Zech 12:10-11)** What a moment in time!

Like when Joseph revealed himself to his brothers in **(Gen 45:3)** announcing "I am Joseph!", resulting in them mourning and weeping at the same time, so it will be with the Jews when Yeshua returns and reveals Himself to them not only as their brother but as their Messiah! What a scene! If there is one other scene on earth that I would want to witness, then it would be this one! Who knows! Just maybe as part of the cloud of witnesses we will be able to view this awesome reunion!

I praise God for Abraham, Isaac and Jacob and all the saints that followed who took hold of the baton of faith handed down to them by Yahweh, keeping their faith and their eyes on the finish line, whilst running this race with perseverance and obedience! No wonder our Lord could triumphantly cry out on the Cross of Calvary, **"It is finished!"** This cry which encompassed all of God's purposes of redemption for mankind, included every promise and prophecy concerning the nation of Israel!

Was it not Joshua who hundreds of years before, after successfully leading the Israelites into the promised land, confidently, triumphantly and prophetically declared, *"Not one of all the LORD'S good promises to the house of Israel failed; every one was fulfilled!"* **(Joshua 21:45)** Yes, All of God's Word is indeed fulfilled in Yeshua Hamashiach, our Lord and Messiah, through whom every child of the Most High God has access to the eternal promised land!

The significance, importance, purpose and power of prayer is nowhere more powerfully displayed than in **Revelation 5:8** (*"Each one had a harp and they were holding* *golden bowls full of incense which were the prayers of the saints")* and **Revelation 8:3-4** *("Another angel, who had a golden censer, came and stood at the altar. He was given much incense to offer, with the prayers of all the saints, on the golden altar before the throne. The smoke of the incense, together with the prayers of the saints, went up before God from the angel's hand).*

It is the scenes in these two chapters that leaves me in no doubt about how much God honors prayer! It is the prayers of the saints in these places of honor in the very throneroom of God Almighty, that has moved His hand through the ages and now plays a role of such significance that in both these chapters, where the prayers of the saints are mentioned, two of the most important events in the Book of Revelation takes place!

Our prayers, like trophies, are displayed on the most glorious and prestigious podiums of all, the altar of grace, in the very throne room of God Almighty! These the prayers of Abraham, Moses, Daniel and

Elijah to mention but a few. These are the simple prayers, the wordless prayers like Hannah's, those heartrenching prayers of pain and tears! These are those sacrificial prayers that we prayed for others when in the valley of our own lives! These are prayers of warfare and prayers of ambition like that of Jabez! These are the intercessions of the saints that have changed lives in homes, communities, cities and nations! These are your prayers and mine!

As we continue co-labouring with our Lord and Saviour in this ministry of intercession, let us never forget the price that was paid on Calvary, forever giving Him thanks for such a glorius salvation, first for the Jew then for the Gentile! *"But Israel will be saved by the LORD with an everlasting salvation; you will never be put to shame or disgraced to ages everlasting."* **(Isaiah 45:17)**

Let us deeply appreciate His precious blood shed for us, giving thanks for the provision that is ours within His blood! From **Exodus 12:13** to **Revelation 12:11** this blood has never lost it's power!

As we daily apply the blood of Yeshua to our own lives may we not forget to apply this blood to the nation of Israel as well, as we committ ourselves to intercede for them until they say,

Baruch Haba B'shem Adonai,

"Blessed is He who comes in the name of the Lord" **Matthew 23:39**

AMEN!

www.ingramcontent.com/pod-product-compliance
Lightning Source LLC
Chambersburg PA
CBHW062002040426
42447CB00010B/1868